Dedication

For my wife Amy, the one person who believes in me and guides me through my tunnel x

For our crazy children Harvey, Louie, Ellie and Austin. I hope my poems make you proud and through my words you'll forever know how much I love you all.

To Ian 'Blocks' Robinson for being my best mate when I needed a best mate the most.

For Jimbo who over 20 years has been a constant source of friendship, support and love.

For Ramona, Molly and Jane Watt, Joanne Milne, Charlotte Dewitt, Sara Evans, David and Rebecca Alexander, Jackie Mcgee and all my Stand By Me RP family

Publishers Information

First published in Great Britain in 2016 by Kissed Off Publications.

This edition was published using CreateSpace. For more information, please contact Kissed Off Publications.

ISBN: 978-1530000401

For more information, and other awareness titles, please contact Kissed Off Publications through our website www.kissedoff.co.uk

Stand by Me RP

Dave Steele

Retinitis Pigmentosa can be a blessing and a curse. Since losing the majority of my sight in the last 2 years I have and still continue to battle everyday with anxiety, fears for my future and the future of my children, acceptance from a world full of misconceptions and constantly having to adjust as my tunnel of sight continues to shrink. Although RP has also blessed me with the ability to realise the important things in life. I know I am never alone with this and have met the most amazing people within the RP and Usher community. Through my blindness I have discovered a new found gift for talking about the things that a lot of us go through when faced with going blind. I have always believed that music and poetry can make an impact, touch the heart and heal the soul in a way like nothing else. I hope this collection of poems can reach those who struggle sometimes with going blind. Help friends and family understand how it can be for us. I hope my poems can help raise awareness so one day the world understands that there are many different shades of blind.

Dave Steele x

My Blind Secret

I have a secret from the world,
that most of you don't know.
Won't hear it in the way I talk
and eyes no clue will show.

If you listen to my story,
something new to learn you'll find.
For though I'm looking straight at
you,
I'm legally blind.

It's not a simple yes or no,
I'm more a shade of grey.
I rarely venture out alone,
as things get in the way.

For what I see affects my days,
in much more ways than one.
And this for some continues,
until little left has gone.

But still this pains invisible,
to those that pass us by.
There's some afraid to hold a
cane,
because of questions why.

Accused of making up our claim
and made to feel a fraud.
Feel drained of all my confidence,
feel trapped behind this door.

Now hardest thing to come to
terms,
that makes my days feel long.
It holds us back,
knowledge they lack,
for all who've got it wrong.

To hear they're judge and jury,
even though their facts aren't
straight.
Feel misdirected fury,
wish opinions now could wait.

To take the time to get to know,
the visions that we share.
Come join me in this tunnel,
hold my hand and show you care.

4

This thing they call RP

I know you've never heard before
of this thing they call RP
So let me help you understand
how it affects people like me

It's always lived inside me from
ancestor's faulty gene
To untrained eye unnoticed lie
remained for years unseen

Whilst in my early twenties
it began to show first trace
I noticed eyes would struggle
moving from dark to light place

But felt I wasn't ready
so this RP I'd deny
No helping hand stick head in
sand
as seeing days pass by

For years I hid it from myself
as wrong as that might be
Till one day it was obvious
that it was hard to see

So off I went to specialist
to take the blindness test
I knew that I would fail them
but that's probably for the best

When doctor's diagnosis came
delivered hard and cold
I may be seeing nothing
by the time that I grow old

It hit me like a hammer
when confirmed what we both
knew
Chance my children were affected
would be simple 1 in 2

The guilt I felt another tear
as I began to grieve
Yet to the outside world
it's difficult to just believe

My blindness creeping inwards
like a speckled hazy tunnel
My grip on independence
vanished
down this darkened funnel.

Began to feel so anxious
every time that I went out
No longer do the simplest things
be filled with fear and doubt

My world was caving in on me
I needed to adjust
I lost some friends and family
I learned just who to trust

I never needed sympathy
Just someone to understand
No need for full time carer
just sometimes a helping hand

I battled for my confidence
I learned to use my cane
I learned to see the best in things
go dancing in the rain

With time my wounds were healing
even though my eyes got worse
Began to write it down for you
through poem song and verse

To fight to raise awareness
for those going blind alone
So through my words our voice be heard
Not isolate at home.

What might be

Every night I close my eyes,
I dream of what might be.
I wonder if tomorrow is the last
day that I see.

I think of times when faces are
just shapes all full of blur.
My children all grown up, but all I
see is how they were.

I long to see how beautiful my
daughter has become.
Or see the man in front of me so
proud to call my son.

My love has eyes that sparkle,
one of many things I miss.
though I can't see their faces,
everyday I'll hug and kiss.

I miss the way they'd smile at me,
I hate I made them cry.
I wish this wasn't happening,
forever thinking why.

But all of this tomorrow, none of
this has happened yet.
For there will still be good times,
that's one thing I'll not forget.

Surround myself with loved ones
and their voices always hear.
Be thankful for all I still have,
they'll be no need for tears.

Stay positive and strong, only
choice to carry on.
Remember all that you have left,
instead of one thing gone.

Make every day a happy one,
but if the bad come back.
Just make sure that you're not
alone,
then depression we'll attack.

So if like me,
one day not see
and sometimes you feel scared.
Just keep these words within your
heart,
and we'll be more prepared.

Disappearing world

My world is disappearing right before my very eyes
and as the tunnel gets much smaller,
another part of me now dies.

Can't believe that this is happening,
never thought it would be me,
for all my trials that I've been through,
in this life certain I'd see.

But it seems I took for granted,
all the days I had full sight,
should have seen so many places,
should have gone out more at night.

Wish I'd looked more at the stars
and all worlds most wondrous things,
now rely on my imagination
for the problems blindness brings.

Still I'm grieving for the future,
ever longing for the past,
waking up each day and wondering
if these sights will be my last.

Know I'm cutting myself off
from the world to spare the pain,
find it hard to see in sunshine,
find it hard to see in rain.

Feel I've lost my place in line,
all because I've fading vision,
but I need to make this fine,
need to make it my life's mission.

Have to build a new foundation,
new direction in my life,
have to do it for my children,
have to do it for my wife.

I will stand up now for others,
who's life's door has firmly shut,
be my sisters and my brothers,
no more days in comfy rut.

Words will open heart and soul,
by showing my example,
focused now on every goal,
feeling brave to take a gamble.

So if days get hard you've played your cards and walls are closing in,
hope these words make sense,
pull down defence,
and you never give in.

Just stand by me and you will see
and blind we'll fight as one,
together sightless friend,
always depend,
long after visions gone.

Future living blind

I'm clinging on to scenes that play
repeating in my mind,
whilst trying not to focus on a
future living blind.

But each and every happy time is
tainted by the thought,
that I'll forget left with regrets as
seeing days cut short.

I watch my wife gaze at me as I'm
playing with my son,
just pray that she will look that
way long after sight has gone.

My children will be proud of me
be never seen as weak,
i'll show them all my poems and
for blind people they speak.

Won't see me as disabled with a
target on my back,
for I'll be strong this world belong
despite one thing I lack.

But these things are the future so
for now I'll bide my time,
and cherish every second always
trust it will be fine.

I know some days I'm distant but
I'm never giving in,
just need to breathe
take time to grieve
won't let the bad days win.

Have faith my words will take me
to a place where I belong,
to reach the ones that need me
writing poems singing songs.

So if you feel I speak for you as I
open up my heart,
Just spread my words around the
world one day I'll get my start.

Tomorrow

Tomorrow I will promise no longer
be held back
Tomorrow won't feel incomplete
for one sense that I lack

Tomorrow I won't stay indoors
no longer be recluse
Tomorrow they will value me
no longer be no use

Tomorrow I will not be scared
to walk alone in crowds
Tomorrow I'll be more prepared
feel confident and proud

Tomorrow they will look at me
and see the man inside
Tomorrow I'll feel valued will be
seen as more than blind

Tomorrow I will see the world
although through blur and haze
Tomorrow I won't feel upset
they'll be no bad eye days

Tomorrow I won't feel alone
when strangers won't believe
Tomorrow I will not be hurt
by those that choose to leave

Tomorrow I will step outside
and proudly use my cane
Tomorrow I'll ignore the stares
no longer feel ashamed

Tomorrow all my fears away
if your strength I can borrow
So maybe it should be today
instead of just tomorrow.

Love is blind

Every day I wake up and I smile
when I see you,
not taking things for granted
as they slowly fade from view.

It gets lonely in this tunnel with
forever closing walls,
but within this dim I let you in you
catch me when I fall.

Each sight my eyes take in now
I cling as time slips past,
forever hold these colours bold in
memories to last.

Days filled with children's laughter
whilst blinded with the sun,
a happy ever after
long past my vision gone.

Nights filled with love and
romance whilst leading me the
way,
my trust in you through grip like
glue your love with me to stay.

On days when I feel darkness
blind panic fills my mind,
you hold me down remove this
frown replace with laughter lines.

Together we'll grow old now
and though my looks may go,
your face won't age behind this
haze 'cause love is blind you
know.

Tunnels collapse

When I awoke this morning,
my vision filled with haze.
I tried to rub them clear and hoped,
I'd have more seeing days.

But darkest fear had happened,
my tunnel had collapsed.
For what was left had faded,
now my visions thing of past.

I looked in to the mirror,
but couldn't see me there.
My face was out of focus
and my mind wasn't prepared.

I had to break to news,
to my wife and family.
How could my children understand,
their dad no longer sees.

I didn't see their faces, but heard
their stifled tears.
I thought we were prepared for this,
since we had known for years.

Then out of darkest panic,
a strength forgot I had.
It filled my heart with positive
and chased away the bad.

Remembered all faces,
blind people I had met.
And even though they'd lost their sight,
they lived with no regret.

Won't let the blindness take me,
still so much I can do.
Begin this life's next chapter,
take my chance to start anew.

I'll feel my way to better days,
my eyes replaced by touch.
For with them here to guide me,
Hands entwined in loved ones clutch.

So if you fear the morning,
when your seeing days will end.
Just know your life's not over
take my strength it's yours to lend.

Visions fight

Arise from darkest slumber,
once more to visions fight.
I know I may have little left,
but try with all my might.

Again I must continue,
make the most of what I've got.
Most days it just comes natural,
but other times it's not.

For me there is no option,
until our eyes can fix.
How long is left of seeing days,
as visions time bomb ticks.

But I won't dwell in future,
regrets will leave in past.
Will make the most of every day,
that pass us by so fast.

So when the blindness gets too much,
sometimes for you to face.
Just start again tomorrow,
with good the bad replace.

Blind love

My love is so protective,
she watches out for me.
She makes sure I get out each
day,
despite this damn RP.

She knows just when to guide me
and when to stand alone.
She even knows when I need
space,
to soul recharge at home.

I know that I can't see that much,
but in her eyes I do.
I see the pride she has in me,
to start each day anew.

She try's to hide her feelings,
the fear that fills her heart.
Though nothing that this
blindness brings,
will tear our love apart.

I know in me she's patient,
as frustration in me grows.
What I find hard to sometimes
say,
one look, I know she knows.

But if she saw the picture,
the sight that now remains.
I'm scared that she would fall
apart,
give in to all that pains.

Our children give us focus,
they lift the haze and blur.
We think of all good things to
come,
not just on how things were.

Although some day in future,
I know I may not see.
In blindness never be alone,
With my love, my family.

Recurring RP dream

As I lay on my pillow,
my mind begins to race.
All thoughts turn to the problems,
that each day I have to face.

Alone here in the darkness,
to sound of ticking clock.
I waste my night times worrying,
how little sight I've got.

But every time I fall in to,
recurring RP dream.
My worries waiting for me here,
replaying every scene.

I try hard to escape them,
but they just pull me back.
My tunnel seems to shrink again,
as negative attacks.

With every morning hope returns,
find strength to carry on.
As long as I have some sight left,
I'll use it best till gone.

I'll focus on the positives,
though blind still got to give.
Each second making memories,
will not forget to live.

Just hope that when my head returns,
to pillow I can sleep.
Not slip in to recurring dream,
where visions left defeat.

The Cure

Today's the day we've waited for,
they say they've found the cure.
We'll see just how the whole world sees,
just like we did before.

We'll jump behind the wheel again,
no stress from A to B.
Our confidence is high once more,
for all the world to see.

From now on they'll be no more tears,
or feeling on our own.
in darkness we will lead the way
and venture out alone.

Those that once abandoned us,
will knock upon our door
and promise to be friend to us unlike they were before.

Our canine friends will have a rest,
a well earned holiday.
'Cause now we see 120 and have put our canes away.

The flashes have now disappeared,
the glare and all the haze.
Replaced by perfect vision,
no more bruises happy days!

No more stares or questions,
or faces look unsure.
Today we'll walk without their gaze, cause now we have our cure.

But all this has me thinking,
should we be the ones to change.
The world has sight but no vision
and no pill can turn that page.

For now it's clear I got it wrong,
this life's not bad I'm sure.
Just try to see what we still see, understanding is the cure.

What will be

The future is a picture,
that none of us can see.
Although it's sometimes difficult,
but what will be will be.

In a world forever fading,
we still have much to give.
Though eyes are blind,
you still might find,
sometimes forget to live.

Some of us may feel distant,
like the world has had enough.
Though we're impaired and some days scared,
we'll talk when things get rough.

So as the days go by now,
don't think of visions gone.
Just cherish what you still can see,
for when you may have none.

Remember we're in this together,
though the tunnel is our own.
Just stand by me, we'll beat RP and never be alone.

Eyes wide shut

Being blind can be so scary,
living days with eyes wide shut.
So we must change minds,
seek out to find,
the ones who've given up.

There are those of us who live in fear
as to what the future holds,
who spend their days
lock themselves away
and it's time their stories told.

Depression can be a symptom
as we grieve for vision gone,
need love of friends and family
but some of us have none.

It's those we must stand up for
to the world we'll shout out loud,
let's fight for each others confidence
we are blind and we are proud.

So if your eyes are fading don't let your spirit slip,
just remember you're amazing
let my words repair the rip.

Walk within my shoes

Imagine for one minute,
you could walk within my shoes.
You would finally understand
there's much more than my sight
to lose.

You would see the friends and
family,
that have sadly walked away.
No patience for my feelings,
so alone in this tunnel I stay.

You would feel the fear inside my
soul, surrounded in a crowd.
The panic and frustration,
when I long to shout out loud.

See the world as judge and jury,
asking how can you be blind.
Quick to make their own mind up,
no answers need to find.

If you truly walked within my
shoes,
could you just control the fear.
As the faces that you see each
day,
began to disappear.

Could you say goodbye to beauty,
to the stars that light the sky.
Future unsure,
no sign of a cure
and still no reason why.

Could you find the strength to
carry on
and put your fears aside.
Treating blindness as one of life's
speed bumps,
but you still enjoy the ride.

After every fall,
carry on stand tall,
like there's nothing left to lose.
But would you have the strength,
go the extra length.
If you walked within my shoes.

21

Behind closed doors

I used to face this on my own,
spend days behind closed doors.
Felt like the world couldn't see me
and no place for me no more.

Now each day to you I talk,
sending words across the globe.
For I can touch the blindest heart,
filling darkened room with hope.

Before the time I first reached out,
I wished someone out there would.
And no matter how loud I'd shout,
never knew without sight I'd feel good.

But to open up my heart to all,
was a gamble that payed off.
So today I now stand proud and tall
and I hold my head aloft.

Though it only seems like yesterday
when invisible I'd be.
Written off by those I needed most
and the world looked right through me.

Even though we all have much to give,
hidden somewhere in our hearts.
Why do some think cause our eyes won't work,
that we can't play our part.

Still to them this pains invisible
and though most won't have a clue.
Just because my eyes,
they don't look blind,
doesn't mean I cope like you.

Cause my vision holds me back each day,
as I try to compensate.
Still the simplest tasks can lead to fear
and for guiding hand I wait.

Though today I feel that bit stronger now,
something's still can't do alone.
I'm so grateful for the company,
wish I could go out on my own.

Watching my independence leave,
was much harder than losing my sight.
Didn't think I'd be made to feel 2nd class,
didn't think they'd have the right.

Some of us refused a taxi home,
just because our friend's a dog.
Why do some still believe
just because they don't know,
that my pride is their's to rob.

Still these things they haven't broken me,
they have made me so much more strong.
Taught me I must now help others,
show them that in this world they belong.

But I wouldn't be now able to,
if I hadn't have first talked to you.
And for every crack that from now on appears,
I know you will be my glue.

Now my future has a brighter end,
even within this tunnel of mine.
Together cane by cane,
you'll be with me,
forever cherished friends online.

Blindman's Best Friend

Today's the day I feared would
come,
the day the lights went out.
The blur and glare has gone away,
my heart is crying out.

The time's arrived I knew it would,
but feel that I'm prepared.
With four legged friend right by
my side,
no reason to be scared.

My heart beats fast
and chest is tight, anxiety sets in.
But soon I'll breathe and know
you're there,
I'll face the world again.

My eyes still have a sparkle,
filled with memories inside.
Of loved ones faces, places, you.
No blindness could deprive.

But future's mine
and hope still holds,
so on adventures new.
So like before,
I'll step once more.
For by my side there's you.

You once returned my confidence
and asked me for your trust.
I let you in my world of dim
and what was choice nows must.

So even though the days now
here,
deep down I will be fine.
For time heals all, nothing to fear.
Your eyes will now be mine.

One Day in the future

One day in the future,
We all will see again.
One day in the future,
I'll rest this weary pen.

The cure that we've all waited for,
at last it will be here.
The faces we've not seen so long,
be met with happy tears.

One day in the future,
blind children will be none.
For first time they will see the
smiles,
of love from dad and mum.

They'll run around without a care,
no need for Braille or cane.
Will always feel included,
not different or ashamed.

One day in the future,
the old won't live in blur.
One day in the future,
they'll see just like before.

In twilight years, no longer fear,
end life alone in black.
There's plenty still,
with magic pill,
their vision will come back.

One day in the future,
I wish would hurry up,
One day in the future,
be soon with any luck.

Blind Panic

This morning I awoke,
from deepest peaceful dream.
I opened up my eyes and things
were not quite as they seemed.

The usual hazy tunnel,
from where I try to see my way.
Had suddenly got smaller,
whilst on comfy pillow lay.

The blurry fog and haze had some
how crept in to the centre.
Felt fear inside my fragile heart,
but now blind panic entered.

Could this be the beginning,
visions end so long I'd feared.
A burden to my family,
again my love's eyes teared.

Was last night the last time,
that face of loved ones I would
see.
Once more began to panic,
screaming "why should this be
me".

But this is a reality that some of
us must face.
Spend days clinging to vision,
then it's gone without a trace.

Though for this day preparing,
I have practiced and I've trained.
So now that it is finally here,
this fear I will contain.

I've fought for independence,
tried my best to this accept.
Till blind I live each day like last,
no future filled regrets.

So when my sight has gone,
I'll still be happy as can be.
For I have still got so much more,
there's more than sight to me.

Words of sight

Speaking from the heart for me,
is a natural thing to do.
I try to write these words of sight,
that relate to me and you .

To speak about depression
or anxiety setting in.
A battle for acceptance,
not to let the negative win.

We all are on a journey,
different time and different stage.
No matter creed or colour,
where we're from or what our age.

The tunnel that we live in,
is a place we can't escape.
We need our super powers,
but we can't find our cape.

No matter where you are,
I hope you know you're not alone.
There's lots of blind friends out
there
and like you we're accident prone.

We may not have a guidance dog
or get around by cane.
We all have different battles,
but our fight for sights the same.

So if this whole things new to you,
worlds ripped apart at seam.
Don't dwell in isolation,
there's a spot upon our team.

A helping hand, some good
advice in poem or in song.
So stand by me and you will find
a place where we belong.

Don't wait for me

Don't wait for me
in darkened room,
use as excuse,
to stay in gloom.

Don't wait for me
pin all your hopes,
as dreams you had
go up in smoke.

Don't wait for me
and waste your days,
as eyes are filled
with cloud and haze.

Don't wait for me
I may not come,
there's challenges
to still be won

Don't wait for me
spend all your time,
thinking scientists
will make you fine.

Don't wait for me
it's not so bad,
there's still good times
to be had.

Don't wait for me
yes I'm the cure,
one day I'll come
but when not sure.

Hand to Touch

Going blind can be so scary,
but it's harder on your own.
It's hard to come to terms with this,
but some are all alone.

I've spoke to those who's social life, through blindness been cut short.
No friends and not much family,
so we need to lend support.

A husband lost,
a partner left,
cause sight loss got too much.
As confidence and vision fades,
they long for hand to touch.

Feel too much of a burden,
to make new romance or a friend.
Through RP you're my family,
so my strength is yours to lend.

Know no ones life is perfect
and we all have day to days.
To show you care won't take a second,
There are lots if different ways.

A kind word or a shoulder,
through the bad times and the good.
Treat everyone how we'd expect,
so blind future is all good.

By My Side

Every time that I go out,
I know I can't see much.
But to my side,
just out of view,
I feel you hand to touch.

You're more than just a guide to me,
keep obstacles at bay.
Although I sometimes can't see you,
your love for me will stay.

They say beauty's in beholders eye,
but yours is in my mind.
For it is clear for all to see,
although I'm going blind.

Each night whilst you're in peaceful dream,
my mind begins to race.
I take in every laughter line,
that's written on your face.

I pray each night when morning comes,
I've one more day to see.
But when the detail fades to grey,
you'll still have love for me.

Through my blind eyes

Do you ever stop and wonder,
what the world looks like to me?
Or how it feels to be held back,
because it's hard too see.

To know that maybe one day soon,
your world could disappear.
Be afraid to step outside your door
and face each trip with fear.

To know that there's something's
you just can't do.
Like jump behind the wheel and drive,
just like when you used to.

My independence slipped right
through my hands.
It seems that since my eyes got
worse,
I've had to change my plans.

I lost my sight and with it
confidence.
I've fought the system to survive,
to me it makes no sense.

How hard is it to get the help we
need.
I spend my days now following,
where once I used to lead.

It hurts the precious family I've
built.
I hope that I've not passed it on,
I live with untold guilt.

I wish that all the world would see
our way.
I'm sick of reading story's of our
guide dogs turned away.

How in this age they still
discriminate.
Information at their fingertips,
it's hard to contemplate.

If you could put a foot inside my
shoe.
Would your eyes see the same as
mine and share my point of view.

Then together they'll be no more
being blind.
For if the world could understand
our bad days will be behind.

Behind the curtain

Living life behind this curtain,
is a challenge everyday.
As time passes by,
days wondering why,
more things seem to get in the
way.

Seems like forever counting these
bruises,
from those trips, stumbles and
falls.
But the more we seem to get it
feels,
the more comes in these walls.

If we could just get to see the big
picture,
just like everyone else simply
does.
Never knowing for sure,
one day we'll have a cure.
Things are clearer and travels no
fuss.

But we can't spend our lifetime
just waiting,
for something that may never
come.
Though we all should have hope,
must make sure that we cope.

After blindness our lives still go
on.
It's life's scars that make us much
stronger
and there's still so much to
achieve.
Not the vision in our eyes,
but the ones in our mind.
That gives us the strength to
believe.

So remember on days when you
panic,
'bout what the future will be.
When eyes come to fail,
it's not the end of your tale.
With time comes acceptance
you'll see.

Come hold my hand

Come hold my hand,
as we stumble in to the darkness.
Walk by my side,
as my world it disappears.
Help me see what's left can still be cherished.
Take my mind off all that's to be feared.

Let my voice be the light to help to guide you.
Hear my song when the fog fills up your eyes.
Feel my words,
on the days you need to feel them.
Be my strength on the days I can't be yours.

Get me out,
in to the world I don't feel part of.
Say I'm wrong to feel that I'm alone.
Close your eyes and imagine they'll never open.
Learn to walk in a new way from before.

Know there's strength in us,
just need reminding.
Call me friend when there's laughter when there's tears.

A letter to the past

I'd like to write a letter,
a letter to myself.
I'd post it back in time to when,
my eyes were in good health.

To days before denial,
when I didn't have a clue.
Before my sight affected me
and all the things I do.

To when I was still driving,
on others not rely.
To time when I was confident,
could see in midnight sky.

I'd tell myself not worry,
'bout things that I can't change.
I'd tell myself bout shades of blind,
so I won't think it's strange.

I'd tell myself don't panic,
for future living blind.
I'd tell myself I don't need sight,
for things I'm yet to find.

I hope that when I read it,
my message won't forget.
I hope that I will take advice,
not give myself regrets.

I hope that I won't isolate,
live days as blind recluse.
Cut myself of from outside world
and think that I'm no use.

Perhaps I shouldn't post it,
have faith I'll find my way.
For what has passed has made
me strong and brought me here
today.

Blind Guilt

How can I let you love me,
when I feel that I'm to blame.
For what I've brought in to our
lives,
the cause of all this pain.

Perhaps if you loved someone
else,
you'd have a stress free life.
No more forever worrying,
no troubles, no more strife.

Our children's future safe from
this,
in life they'd always see.
Just some of darkest thoughts
that sometimes live inside of me.

I know that they are wrong to
think,
have no place in my mind.
They seem to be a symptom
as Im slowly going blind.

I know because you love me,
that you share in all my fears.
Just wish I wasn't causing,
all your upset,
all your tears.

Within my heart a pain lives there,
an overwhelming guilt.
It's slowly tearing down the walls,
our family carefully built.

Just know that all these doubts I
have,
won't be around forever.
They reappear without a sign,
they change just like the weather.

Although I wouldn't change a
thing,
if one day there's a cure.
But that's the hardest part of
living life whilst so unsure.

Cause no one seems to
understand,
what going blind is like.
They've formed their own
opinions
and feel as if they're right.

They're quick to judge,
in crowds won't budge,
although I hold my cane.
Yet wonder why so many feel,
that we're the ones to blame.

So as my dark thoughts slip away,
my mind now turns to you.
to find the words to help you and
refresh your soul a new.

To know it's only natural, to feel
this way sometimes.
I'll share with you my darkest
days and pray that we'll be fine.

Set the record straight

I think it's time we set things straight,
it's time we all spoke out.
To let the world around us know
what blindness is about.

To help the ones who question
as they look in to our eyes,
who fail to see that some still see
and we're not telling lies.

To those of us who live in fear
of being out alone,
Won't use a cane and feel ashamed
so stay trapped in our home.

It's time to find a treatment
that no doctor could give,
so now let's speak as one voice
for those who forgot to live.

Now blind we'll find each other
from all corners of this land,
to step out of the darkness to make them understand.

#RPlikeme

I thought that I was all alone,
I thought how could this be
There must be others out there,
who have RP just like me.

But no ones ever heard of this,
In circle friends of mine,
How could they spot the
symptoms,
when it's hard to see the signs.

I tried to talk about it,
but I don't know what to say.
I'm full of bumps and bruises,
from all things now in the way.

But then a flood of pictures,
all across computer screen,
So many different faces,
felt like best thing I have seen.

All corners of the world,
with eyes now just the same as
mine,
although they're slowly dying,
none of them have lost there
shine.

Their stories touched my heart
and soul,
felt good to hear them share.
I've found my RP family
it's good to know they're there.

So if you've one time said the
words,
"no one understands".
You've no longer got that excuse,
call out we'll take your hand.

For if you're in a tunnel
and you're struggling to see.
Just type in to your keyboard
#RPlikeme.

Time Machine

I wish I had a time machine,
to future I would go.
I'd sneak in to the years from now,
to when the world would know.

The cure for all our faulty genes,
that robs us of our senses.
Repair our eyes with stem cells,
rebuilding our defences.

I'd bring the answers back to us,
so we'd no longer wait.
Wouldn't struggle with the day to
day,
or get ourselves in state.

Our eyes that look so normal,
Would inside be nice and clear.
Nothing for us to come to terms,
no need to shed a tear.

They'd come to me from near and
far,
blind people young and old.
I'd lead them from the darkness,
to a world of colours bold.

The children who've been blind
since birth,
have never seen their mum.
No longer need for sunglasses,
whilst walking in the sun.

But this is just a day dream,
though I know it's soon our fate.
Without my special time machine,
guess we'll just have to wait.

For my wife

Another day begins will it be clear
or it be haze,
I start each day wondering bout
the challenges I'll face,

but you are there as you always
are to gently take my hand,
to lead me where I cannot see
and show you understand.

Where others keep their distance
you just listen for a while,
I hear your voice and instantly
nothing to do but smile,

your my best friend to that no end
you share with me you life,
I now depend, darkness descends
but you are still my wife.

The days pass by in blink of eye
but we are on a mission
to fill our children's days with love
no sight but lots of vision

For as to what the future holds
who know but one things certain,
with you inside my heart and soul
I'll see right through this curtain.

Some days I may feel far from you
like tortoise in a shell
Solemn retreat but when I speak
it's you my fears I tell

For with this ring no blindness
thing we'll never let it beat us
as long as there's a voice I'll sing
with you it can't defeat us

Give me my pride and see inside
the man you love and We'll wish,
from days of blue we'll start a new
our future we will cherish

Forget our worth

How could I just not see the thing,
that's right in front of me.
Whilst I was busy going blind,
lost what I used to be.

Forgot what makes me different,
from everybody else.
When anything would go wrong,
I would try to blame myself.

How could I be so blind,
to just lose track all my worth.
I listened to their chorus,
but forget to sing the verse.

Spent too much time on people,
who told me what I couldn't do.
The truth now Is I've finally learned,
that most don't have a clue.

I couldn't just keep quiet,
after what I heard them say.
To reach out now to others,
just like me in many ways.

The world seems so much smaller,
for the ones who have RP.
So many things that I have learned,
like some who are blind still see.

I heard so many stories,
from the ones who can't speak out.
I'll lend my voice to others,
spread awareness with a shout.

They may not listen straight away,
but they will know the tune.
And if they keep on listening,
they'll understand us soon.

Then there will be no reason,
for the blind to feel apart.
We may not have good eyesight,
but with vision it's a start.

No one should feel ashamed,
to use a cane or use a dog,
It's their minds that are clouded,
think it's time we lift the fog.

So if you're feeling incomplete,
just know you're not alone.
Remember there's a strength in us,
if lost can be regrown.

Blind Frustration

I'm feeling a frustration,
build up inside of me.
I'm tired of all the accidents
from things I fail to see.

Most people think I'm clumsy,
just need to take more care.
As no one seems to understand
and all they do is stare.

The confidence I used to have
grows less and less each day.
To blindness journey I progress
as more sight slips away.

But no one has the answers
they've yet to find the cure.
Feel terrified my futures set
end days in haze and blur.

I feel I'm running out of time
till what I've left is gone.
But I know I will find a way
through blindness carry on.

I'm secretly preparing,
for days when I can't see.
I try to spare my worry,
from my precious family.

Forever fighting guilt I have,
of what it's done to them.
Waste too much time in what
might be, instead of until then.

The symptoms are invisible,
leave those I know confused.
Feel every stranger doubting,
expecting me to prove.

Some days I feel my eyes can see,
then RP pulls me back.
Another of cruel symptoms,
as retinas attacked.

Inside my fear is growing,
spend more days now at home.
The hardest part of this disease
is feeling all alone.

But that gives me a reason,
to tell you all my fears.
Hope those that feel the same as me,
no longer hide their tears.

There's strength to talk of weakness,
admit to days in need.
Together share times good and bad,
in every word you read.

Around the bend

If tomorrow when I wake up
is the day when I can't see
Will my heart begin to panic
or stay positive in me

If the faces there in front of me
unfocused filled with blur
Will I hold it all together
learn to cope with the unsure

If tomorrow I can't see your smile
for now I'm totally blind
Will I hold on to the memories
I've saved up in my mind

If tomorrow I just fall apart
when all that's left is gone
Will I find the strength within me
to get up and carry on

If tomorrow is the day
when my tunnel fades to black
Will I waste my days just hoping
that a cure some day bring back

If I'm faced with toughest
challenge
to adapt to sightless days
Will I take the help from others
or alone consumed by haze

If tomorrow is the day
when I no longer can see you
Will my heart be forever broken
or find ways to love anew

If tomorrow some day happens
I know it won't be the end
There's more to life than seeing
still so much around the bend

Early Days

I want to tell my children,
all about my early days.
When I could see like everyone,
enjoyed the sunshine's Rays.

The world it felt so different then,
I travelled without care.
Getting round was just so easy,
I'd run down darkened stairs.

I felt so independent,
as I moved from place to place.
The centre of the party,
always smile upon my face.

My worries were so trivial,
just normal day to day.
I never knew that later,
all my sight would fade away.

If ever person blind passed by,
never noticed, never see.
How could I know the same was soon a future meant for me.

I wonder if they saw me,
as the man I was before.
They'd long for me to stay that way,
or know I'm so much more.

They'd wish I was like everyone,
or proud for what can't see.
I try to be good parent,
even though I'm VIP.

I know one day they'll read this
and I pray and hope they can.
Then they will see although I can't,
it's made a stronger man.

So even though my sight has gone
I'll always be your Dad.
I wish we could play football
and that sometimes makes me sad

But I will always love you
that's one thing blindness can't change
and if one day I see again,
you'd probably think it strange.

Just know in life there's challenges,
it's what good person make.
For every turn, a thing to learn for every day we wake.

But I know I have taught you well,
you've learned a lot from me.
You'll always see in others more than disability.

Good Days

Today's one of my good days,
my eyes let in more sight,
my head is free of worry and I'm
comfy in this light.

My confidence is high now
and I'm eager to get out,
feel I'm ready for the problems
that most times fill me with doubt.

I may get my bumps and bruises,
but I'll take them in my stride,
cause today I see the truth is,
I've no reason left to hide.

I won't listen to the voices,
as they talk behind my back,
won't hear their words, now I'll be
heard, awareness they won't lack.

Cause today I'll change opinions,
different ways that we all see,
some see loved ones through a
pin hole,
still no cure for this RP.

There are some of us with Usher,
living Deaf as well as Blind,
wanting world to hear our every
fear
for future in our minds.

They won't offer us their pity,
for today they'll get to know,
we are confident and witty,
can do more than most will show.

So today's one of my good days,
hope tomorrow same will be,
but in back of mind,
I know I'll find,
that soon I may not see.

But for now no thoughts of future,
for this day today I'll live,
won't live in past
I pray this lasts
be blind and positive.

RP Friends

Why do some of us struggle
our independence we still lose
We live with misconceptions
always so much left to prove

Just because sometimes we need
our canes doesn't mean that we
can't see
Life's hard with no peripheral
just one symptom of RP

I know there's many out there
going blind behind closed doors
It's time we put an end to this
shouldn't happen anymore

The world should know our story
many shades of losing vision
We'll fight for blindness glory
Raise awareness that's our
mission

To hope one day we're valued
without feeling sympathy
We have so much still to offer
despite what we can't see

I've spent my days in darkness
feeling lonely and despair
I won't let this now continue
I'll find the ones who care

and together we will set things
straight
so this isolation ends
though for future cure
we all still wait
You are all my RP friends

Tunnels same as mine

I remember when I first was told,
one day I may go blind
And as I searched
the answers were so difficult to
find.

Never heard of this disease
before,
all my friends they had full sight.
Thought that none of them had
noticed,
as I struggled in low light.

For years I'd not give second
thought,
as I'd bump and trip and fall.
I just thought I was clumsy
and that someone moved that
wall.

Guess I was in denial,
for what was still to come.
Spent days behind dark glasses,
as they hurt from slightest sun.

But it was far too easy just to hide
away my fears.
For I had read
and doctors said,
it wouldn't happen yet for years.

But then one day I noticed,
that a fog had filled my head.
My eyes would get so tired
and my mind hurt when I read.

When moving through a crowd
these days,
I'd start to feel unsafe.
Began to not go out as much,
was quickly losing faith.

No longer could deny it,
knew I had to see someone.
But they couldn't give me
answers,
how long till my vision's gone.

They didn't even tell me,
there's a chance I'd feel depressed.
For I would lose more than my
sight,
my life was such a mess.

Then as the weeks and months
passed by,
new skills I had to learn.
Though it was hard,
been dealt my cards,
my confidence returned.

I fought to use the cane now hold,
I fought to use my dog.
They guide and they protect me,
through this ever falling fog.

Although the future scares me
still,
I know that it's ok.
Because I have friends to talk to
now,
understand my darkest day.

For I have many like me,
see blind future, see blind past.
Our bond will not be broken,
our friendship always last.

So if the fears you hold inside,
refuse to see the signs.
You'll never be alone again,
cause your tunnels same as mine.

Last Day

If you knew this was the last day,
before you lost your sight.
Would you spend it in the
darkness,
or making memories in the light.

Would you look in to your loved
ones eyes,
without the slightest blink.
Or would you lock yourself away,
consumed by bad thoughts that
you think.

Would you only see the beauty,
for all the world can bring.
Or would you stay gripped by
depression, only notice the
negative things.

Would you seek one last
adventure,
before the light comes to an end.
Or alone walk in to darkness,
cause you've pushed away your
friends.

Let eyes record their every sight,
from sunrise to sunset.
Or stay safe in denial, whilst trying
to forget.

Would feel as if you were
prepared,
for what may come tomorrow.
Or spend your days alone and
scared,
drowning in your sorrow.

I hope the same as me you'll pick,
as our sight comes to an end
As time pass by with every tick,
for what's around the bend.

Holding on

I love the smiles that greet me,
from my children and my wife.
Each morning I'm so thankful,
that I have them in my life.

For everyday I'm holding on,
to memories we make.
It's getting so much harder,
as my sight this blindness takes.

The first thing on my mind,
as each and everyday begins.
Is will they have to lose theirs too,
a price for all my sins.

I have to block it out,
so I can somehow carry on.
Just trying not to think of times,
when all I see is gone.

I miss my independence,
miss my freedom, miss my car.
I long for days gone by,
when on my own I'd travel far.

Not needing any help,
no need to ask for charity.
Not danger to myself
and all the hazards I can't see.

The simple things no longer do,
like taking out my son.
Just one of countless things,
that makes me feel like blindness
won.

But I can't let them beat me,
I will try and find new ways.
For as long as I keep strong,
I will be fine as vision fades.

Though some days I can't do it,
feel sometimes it's just too much.
But you can take it all away,
with just the slightest touch.

You've seen me at my worst,
and always seem to stick around.
On journey in to blindness
seems together we are bound.

So even when my world is
blurred,
in my mind I'll see you clear.
To share in all life's ups and
downs,
no need to see to know you're
near.

Invisible

Somedays I just don't see things
and other days I do.
It's part of this RP you see,
though most won't have a clue.

My symptoms are invisible,
some think that they are fake.
They don't know how it makes life
hard,
from moment that I wake.

Some people think I'm ignorant,
they think that I ignore.
They think that I've been drinking,
'cause I didn't see that door.

I hear them talk about me,
like sometimes that I'm not there.
They try to take my confidence,
it feels like they don't care.

These days see through a pin
hole,
feel glare at slightest light.
Engulfed by total blackness,
if I'm ever out at night.

I wish I could do all the things,
one time I used to do.
Being blind is not so black and
white,
I wish that they all knew.

Some think that though I still can
read,
it mustn't be that bad.
So many misconceptions here,
it sometimes makes me mad.

I try to live life positive,
I'll beat this unseen pain.
Although at times don't feel it,
I'll go dancing through this rain.

Sometimes I feel frustrated,
for every single trip.
As I feel stress,
and see less,
my eyes take another dip.

But if the world would
understand,
then one day they might see.
There's so much more to us
than our invisible disability.

No Negative

They tried to tell me not to talk
about the negative
Deny to all that it exists in how
some of us live

Can't mention all the bad days
we don't have from time to time
and if you share your problems
then
they're not the same as mine

They said to me the negative
should always be blocked out
Should always show what we can
do
and not the things we doubt

They told me not to open up
for fear of seen as weak
and raise awareness or of
misconceptions never speak

They hoped that I would not
speak out
or bare my deepest scars
My fears about my future how I
long to see the stars

But I put my heart on the line
share blind days bad and good
To others who same stage as me
my story understood

Though if my world is different
to how you learn to cope
can still take from each other
and to them we'll offer hope

The sign of real strength is
showing it's ok to cry
for anyone who says the don't
To you and their self lie

Not interested in sympathy
or making personal gain
I know now that the bluest sky
comes after darkest rain

Always Around

The world today moves quickly,
we rush from here to there.
For others we don't have the time,
to think about or care.

The news is full of story's,
of tragedy and doom.
We hear of people suffering,
It's hard to lift the gloom.

But there must be an answer,
this negative defeat.
Together is the only way,
that we will not be beat.

I maybe losing vision,
but what I've left is clear,
My RP friends are far away,
but they all feel so near.

From here I'm so connected,
to all who know my fears.
We share each others laughter,
we share each others tears.

We talk about inclusion,
so we don't feel alone.
We share our thoughts and
feelings,
so friends and family know.

We fight to raise awareness,
to make the whole world think.
Show how it is to cling to sight,
to teeter on the brink.

To live each day in hope of,
a treatment still to find.
To not forget our real worth,
whilst slowly going blind.

So when our world gets faster,
step back and slow it down.
Appreciate in darkest times,
blind friends always around.

A place we long to see

Today I said goodbye
to what I could see yesterday.
My tunnel little smaller, once
again sight slips away.

I'm now a bit more hesitant,
as I slowly move around.
I don't know where it went to,
but I hope it's one day found.

The little that I could see just
became a little less.
I try to do the simplest things,
but seem to make more mess.

Can't see what's right in front of
me,
till it hits me in the face.
My independence disappeared,
I fight to keep my place.

When love leans in to kiss me,
beauty's face is all a blur.
I wish my vision could go back,
to how it was before.

The thought of being old and frail ,
end days as total blind.
It fills my head and heart with
fear,
a poison in my mind

I want to watch my children grow
and see all they achieve.
I hope that they won't pity me,
a strength in me believe.

A world more understanding,
just how losing sight can be.
A future built on tolerance,
a place we long to see.

But all of these are pipe dreams,
just a fleeting hope for change.
A future where we see once more,
to some that would be strange.

So until then you'll find me here,
as all I see still fades.
I'll hide solitary tear,
behind my darkened shades.

While your asleep

Late at night while you're asleep,
I lie here wide awake.
I memorise the images, this RP try's to take.

The faces of our children,
the laughter in their eyes.
My cheeks are wet,
must not forget,
as vision slowly dies.

The beauty of a summers day,
the sight of winters chill.
We pray for us it will return,
come back with magic pill.

The look of love that's in your eyes,
when you look back at me.
Each night I wish that it's still there,
when I wake up to see.

These pictures that I take in,
I cling to in my mind.
I save them up for days to come,
for when I'm totally blind.

But tomorrow when I wake up,
these worries will not speak.
Stay focused of the strengths I have,
not those that make me weak.

I'll spend each waking hour,
tell world of RP's fate.
Through poetry and music,
our life's they'll contemplate.

But when the day is over,
to pillow I'll return.
To take in every inch of you,
your face in memory burn.

Our blind life

I feel like I am falling, to the
bottom of the sea.
The world I view gets smaller,
disappears in front of me.

I try swim back to the top,
it's hard to catch my breath.
But everyday gets further away,
to test the strength I've left.

Don't want to feel cut off,
from all the people that I know.
But seems these days the less I
see, less places I can go.

Suspicion when our eyes connect,
that "how can he be blind"
Most people just don't
understand, although they're
always kind.

My tunnelled sight is closing in,
feel soon it maybe gone.
But vision is a different thing,
I'm blessed for some have none.

Appreciate the beauty,
in the simplest things each day.
But now there's more to miss,
as my sight quietly slips away.

So I'll keep on adjusting,
learn to change as I progress.
I'll try to remain positive,
stay focused on this test.

My heart I'll bare, see every tear,
so others aren't alone.
And maybe change some hearts
and minds,
our blind life will be known.

Blindness Clutch

Blind love can be so fragile,
like tender rope that's frayed.
My insecurities pull us down,
crack foundations that we've
made.

For in my heart you're perfect
and it's obvious I'm not.
But why should you be held back,
by this condition that I've got.

I know that you still love me,
but this RP you despise.
I feel a guilt inside at times,
can't look you in the eyes.

I want you to be happy,
your future dreams fulfilled.
Not living as my carer,
your hope by blindness killed.

Although I know I'm stupid,
for thinking all these things.
They bounce around inside my
brain and off it's walls they ping.

Think would you be much better,
with another who can see.
With someone who could lead the
way,
not follow just like me.

I've heard of these things happen,
for others got too much.
They've ran away and left their
love,
escaping blindness clutch.

Just pray it doesn't happen,
with me you'll always stay.
Just one of sometimes doubts I
have,
Whilst here in darkness lay.

It's not that I don't love you,
It's just the opposite.
We walk this tunnel hand in hand,
with love you keep it lit.

So If ever love is over,
you spread your wings and fly.
My love for you I'll cling on to,
as seeing days pass by.

Blind practice

Everyday I practice for when I'll
no longer see.
I hone my skills in secret,
nobody knows but me.

I walk around with curtains drawn
and all the lights turned out.
Try not to knock things over,
as I slowly move about.

I don't know if it's working,
but I need to feel prepared.
Can't face a future going blind,
if I'm alone and scared.

So I will keep on learning,
how to cope without my eyes.
And when the day is finally here,
it won't be such surprise.

Draw the line

I want to tell a story,
of how it goes for some.
I used to find it hard in dark,
these days it's hard in sun.

The blur and haze that's in my eyes, crept up on me through time.
I wasted nights spent worrying,
now it's time to draw a line.

For although my sight still leaves me,
my blind future I'll learn to accept.
As for those who once failed to believe me,
I will finally win their respect.

So for all who've been misjudged before,
'cause they couldn't see past what they call.
We are more than disability,
we will gather our strength from each fall.

So in future when we stumble,
then the others like us lead the way.
The support that I see makes me humble.
In the arms of blind community lay.

When lights goes out,
eyes sparkle dies.
I will learn to embrace living blind.
For all the things I no longer see,
will be safe in the back of my mind.

For our children

I've held your hand since the day you were born,
I've been there from the start.
Though see your face through blur and haze,
I feel you in my heart.

But as you grow so does my guilt,
of what might give to you.
I'm told you have my smile and nose,
just pray not my vision too.

The doctors said no way to tell,
all we can do is wait.
Hear mother cry,
as she gaze in eye,
trying to see your fate.

As tears fall down upon your cheek,
with love so true and pure.
If one day your eyesight is weak,
I hope they have found your cure.

But for today,
we'll watch you play and protect you from this burden.
Hope you'll be fine
and show no sign,
cause nothing is for certain.

So just incase,
you take my place in disability.
I'll show you all things you can do, even if you can not see.
I'll change the world for ever,
educate with song and verse.
Make every blind life for the better,

We are different but no worse.
Though blind you'll see there's no limit,
to what you can achieve.
I'll help to build the strength in you,
when you need it to believe.

No longer world will hold you back,
cause of slowly fading vision.
For every challenge we'll attack,

I'll make it my life's mission.
Still odds are only 1 on 2,
my fingers firmly crossed.

And if my blindness pass to you,
ambition won't be lost.
So although it breaks my heart in two,
thinking one day you might not see.
I will fight for all who lose their sight,
make you all my family.

Fade to grey

These days they can seem kind of hard,
as I see less and less.
It seems the more my vision fades,
the more increases stress.

Sometimes the light it hurts my eyes
and so inside I stay.
Another brick within the wall,
that keeps the world at bay.

For as the faces fade to grey,
the more they seem to leave.
Just common trait of blindness fate,
for those who won't believe.

How some can see across a room,
but still not see a hand.
Is one of just a hundred things,
that they don't understand.

Like why do I now use a cane,
or dog to lead the way.
Though I still see,
in front of me,
it's harder every day.

But whist I wait to find a match,
new companion to bring home.
My life it seems to be on hold,
I can't go out alone.

So with these words,
my voice be heard,
as I try to change you views.

This tunnel wouldn't be so dark,
if we had less to prove.
Maybe one day,
I hope and pray,
my words the world will read.
So I'll still write, when there's no light,
for those of us in need.

In the Middle

It seems to me
it's harder for the ones who still cling on.
Who fight as their sight slips away, than those of us who've none.

The picture that bit smaller,
than it was just yesterday.
And all the while we hide our thoughts
and keep them locked away.

Constantly adjusting,
till a time no longer see.
Never thought that I would struggle with simple mobility.

How smallest trip must now be planned
and fills my mind with stress.
And things I'd take for granted now, become a tougher test.

Then just as I have finally learned,
my eyesight takes a dip.
It seems of late, cruel twist of fate,
another RP trick.

In daytime just a change of light,
can knock me off my stride.
Forever falling over things appearing from the side.

As nighttime falls,
behind these walls,
no longer venture out.
One more of unseen sorrow,
of what this RP is about.

As haze descends and good sight ends,
must find a brand new way.
To make our way around this world and find beauty in every day.

We'll learn to look for positive,
in everything we do.
For once you've done,
you'll find you've won
and maybe others will be like you.

Still they'll be days
when you feel as if
you can't go on to fight.
When everything hurts,
you lose your worth,
retreat away from light.

When these days appear,
please no longer fear,
just look for others who like me.
Who have had to lose their vision for the world to truly see.

They say it's those
with the largest wounds,
who have the biggest hearts.
Just hope the world will see it soon,
then we'll all get a new start.

So remember for every sight you lose,
there are things there still to win.
And the day you finally realise,
eyes healing will begin.

Going blind alone

I try to open up my heart,
in everything I write.
Admit I still awake from nightmares,
in the middle of the night.

I hope that if I tell you all my fears,
of how my life can be.
When sight you lack, you won't hold back
and do the same with me.

See the thought of others out there, who are going blind alone.
Fill my nights with dread,
as I lay in bed,
writing poems on my phone.

I'm lucky to have my wife and kids,
blessed with beautiful family.
But though I'm blessed there's more faces,
one day I wish I still could see.

It's for those of us still out there,
on their own still shut away.
Who I fight to reach, hope my words will teach,
I'll be friend no matter what time of day.

Whether just a simple message, that will take away the gloom.
Or a poem that can talk
while your alone there in your room.

Know that I'll be there,
this blind man cares
and I'll make the whole world see.
Just all the misconceptions
and how there's lots of us like me.

How being blind to lots of us,
not total darkness days.
It's more like looking through a straw
and seeing in a haze.

It's knowing that our eyes get worse,
with every day that pass.
The feeling that we've been misjudged,
'cause you're afraid to ask.

So I still write, though hurts this light
and the pain swirls in my head.
But words spill out from darkest dream, as I lay here in my bed.

I hope my words continue,
to bring smiles to those like me.
And say the things you need to say,
to our friends and family.

So no more misunderstanding, no more suffering alone.
Still I will be around for you,
singing song or writing poem.

Grateful

As I opened my eyes this morning,
and light came stinging in.
I know that I am grateful for,
the sight I fight to win.

My loved ones faces for today,
I'll memorise in mind.
And see the places that maybe one day seem hard to find.

So if you catch me glancing,
with a sparkle in my eyes.
I'm just holding on,
till the day comes
to when my vision dies.

Not spending every second feeling bad for what I've lost.
Just cherishing the moments,
for the price my RP cost.

Though it's easy to feel bad,
most days I'm positive.
Cause since my eyes began to go,
I remembered how to live.

If you close your eyes for just one minute,
you'll find you'll pay attention.
To all the things you missed before,
feel things that most won't mention.

I know it's easier to focus on,
the things that make you sad.
But I'll see more without my eyes
and life won't be that bad.

My sight sometimes distracts me from the most important things.
No longer hide,
what I see inside,
with blindness beauty brings.

I understand that though life's changed,
I'll always carry on.
Know I have won more than I've lost,
have gained more than has gone.

So I for one will appreciate,
this fragile gift called sight.
But as I prepare for days without,
I finally see the light.

I've many friends who still today,
my face have never seen.
And though can't miss what they've never had,
or what has never been.

They teach me how to find a strength, that's hiding there within.
For as the time for seeing ends,
a new one will begin.

What's in store

Last night while you were
sleeping,
I lay there wide awake.
Thinking bout the things that we
both have,
that blindness still to take.

My heart is fit to bursting,
how grateful I've become,
I count the simplest blessings,
as I watch our children run.

Although each day it's harder,
as still the blur creeps in.
I try to hold my head up high,
won't let the fears I have win.

My confidence gets knocked still,
there's cuts upon my knee.
My view is getting smaller,
but I'm as happy as can be.

I'm busy making memories,
for days when blind is set.
I'll cram them all inside my head,
so your face I'll not forget.

I'll memorise each wrinkle,
all the flaws you say you hate.
You claim they're imperfections,
to me they make you great.

The smallest of life's details,
one day I'll miss the most.
These gifts each day I celebrate,
appreciate and toast.

So whilst you lay there dreaming,
for me the time goes slow.
I pray I'll see tomorrow,
but I really just don't know.

But until my sights no longer,
through ever shrinking straw.
I'll make the most of what I see,
no matter what's in store.

Against the ropes

When everything is fading,
from these two poorly eyes.
It's no wonder that the strength I've left,
decreases in its size.
When all my daily battles,
hit hard and reach their peak.
The walls around me crumble and leave me feeling weak.

I'm fighting for my vision,
I'm fighting for blood.
I'm fighting for daughter, just like a father should.
But there's too much inside my heart,
for me to learn to cope.
I've lost my fight in going blind,
my backs against the ropes.

A daddy's girl forever,
I thought you'd always be.
One more of life's surprises,
I thought I'd always see.
But you from me been taken,
another in my place.
To join the line as eyes decline,
another fading face.

I'm fighting for my vision,
I'm fighting for blood.
I'm fighting for daughter, just like a father should.
But there's too much inside my heart,
for me to learn to cope.
I've lost my fight in going blind,
my backs against the ropes.

My side and untold story,
that you're too young to know.
A pain aside from going blind,
that I can't watch you grow.
I know you'll know in future,
by then it's much too late.
When all my sight is fading,
entwined in RP's fate.

I'm fighting for my vision,
I'm fighting for blood.
I'm fighting for daughter, just like a father should.
But there's too much inside my heart,
for me to learn to cope.
I've lost my fight in going blind,
my backs against the ropes.

But I won't let this knock me out,
won't take a count of ten.
For when I hear tomorrow's bell,
stand up and fight again.
Although my visions fading fast,
my love for you will not.
I maybe blind forever find,
I'll give you all I've got.

I'm fighting for my vision,
I'm fighting for blood.
I'm fighting for daughter, just like a father should.
Though there's too much inside my heart,
Tomorrows a new day .
I've lost my fight in going blind,
but I'll still find a way.

Good times to be had

I remember pictures,
of times from yesterday.
Before my eyes filled up with blur
and vision slipped away.

I remember faces,
my children's smiling eyes.
The look of love forever stay,
although my visions dies.

I remember colours,
of oceans crystal blue.
They live in hear with every tear,
next to memories about you.

I remember thinking,
I'd watch us both grow old.
Though I won't see your face
again,
your hands still mine to hold.

I remember praying,
that I would learn to cope.
Not dwell on past,
how long will it last,
as plans go up in smoke.

I remember wishing,
they'd take it all away.
My vision treat,
pull down this sheet,
keep blindness now at bay.

I remember feeling,
all I could be is scared.
But now this thing has done its
worst,
I'm feeling more prepared.

I remember crying,
on days my eyes were bad.
But now they're gone I realise,
good times can still be had.

Another Day

My eyes they open slowly,
and the light comes stinging in.
Another day of vision, haven't let
this blindness win.

I feel the glare so quickly, as the
light it pains my head.
But rather now it hurt me,
than to hide away in bed.

But I am just so grateful, that I see
another day.
I have the fight inside of me,
to keep RP at bay.

Won't think about tomorrow,
or if it will be my last.
Won't worry about the future,
or live stuck in days gone past.

I'll put my fears behind me,
every challenge I'll take on.
I'll fight the misconceptions,
until all of them are gone.

Where prejudice still practiced
against disability,
I'll show them understanding,
help them see the world we see.
In my battle with blindness,

I have learnt so many things.
Won't let RP define us,
changing minds with words I
sing.

But if tomorrow when I wake,
the last of sight has gone.
Inside I'll still have vision for this
fight to carry on.

Black and White

There are many others out there,
who have RP just like me.
We face a daily battle,
as we lose our fight to see.

Trying to rely,
on what's impossible to fix.
We look like we can see ok,
just one of RP's tricks.

We live in hazy tunnel,
see the world through smallest straw.
I've spent my days like others have,
alone behind closed door.

At times feel isolation,
had to give away my pride.
To take the help I need,
just so my days not spent inside.

Though when I get outside,
there's still so much I have to face.
Most people don't give second thought,
world moves at fastest pace.

I wish that people understood,
I wish some weren't so cruel
A little girl told not to bring,
her white cane in to school.

We hear the endless stories,
tired of fighting for inclusion.
I thought it would be simple,
but it seems there's some confusion.

Like those of us with guide dogs,
asked to leave our local store.
It's time we raised awareness,
It's time they knew the law.

Just think if it was your child blind,
how would you want the world to treat.
Still when you see an old blind man,
you forget to give up your seat.

I wish that I could help those people going blind alone.
A friendly voice to be there,
at the other end of phone.

It's why I write these poems,
It's why I write these songs.
Just because our visions fading fast,
we all should still belong.

So if you know someone like me,
quickly losing sight.
Don't fall for misconceptions,
It's not always black and white.

Behind my loved ones eyes

If you take a closer look, behind
my loved ones eyes.
You'll find a pain inside there,
the place where RP hides.

A dotted cloud of pigment,
that robs him of his sight.
See's nothing in the faintest dark
and hurts by glare of light.

The world a shrinking tunnel,
that shrinks forever more.
A face, a place, a star filled sky,
to see like once before.

A time of independence, not
others to rely.
Frustrated lack of confidence,
need help to just get by.

These things they all upset him,
I wish they'd disappear.
I wish one day in years to come,
behind his eyes were clear.

A time when worlds opinions,
of how a blind man looks.
Won't be of eyes a vacant,
they'll all have read his book.

They'll hear him speak for others,
who've yet to find their voice.
A fight for blind inclusion,
for what is must not choice.

He writes his deepest feelings,
finds strength to speak of fear.
I'm by his side through changing
tide,
we share the sweetest tear.

But if you look at my loves face,
in just a fleeting glance.
Won't see this cruel condition,
why he'll no longer dance.

A truer word unspoken,
judge book not by it's cover.
The same for those with RP,
I know just ask my lover.

RP's Curse

Daylight flickers far away, across the darkened room.
Reminder of the outside world,
whilst I lay in my tomb.

A stinging pain that won't subside,
brought on by too much stress.
The reason that you find me here,
my eyes are such a mess.

My head it throbs and eye balls swell,
all down to RP's curse.
Seems for today it's got me down,
I'm feeling at my worst.

No medicine can take away the pain that's in my head.
So here in darkened room I lay,
curled up inside my bed.

But later on in my own time,
I'll rise again once more.
Determined not to live my life,
behind my RP door.

I know sometime in future
to my darkened room return.
To lay a while recuperate, as slightest light eyes burn.

Every day I love you back

Life can be so lonely,
when there's nothing in your view.
It's why I count my blessings,
everyday since I found you.

A love like yours for most is just
so difficult to find.
I know how lucky I am in love,
although I'm going blind.

Your features maybe all a blur,
but how I feel is clear.
A never ageing beauty,
in my mind forever dear.

When bad eye days rear ugly
head,
you know just what to say.
Feel love in every word that's said,
you take my breath away.

So many things still I can do,
though on you I depend.
Don't need my sight to support
you too,
your heart and soul defend.

A warm embrace, caress your
face on days when things get
rough.
For in my arms you're always safe,
I'll polish out that scuff.

We all have bumps and bruises
and there's some the eyes can't
see.
We battle our depressions laced
with damn anxiety.

But side by side we'll walk life's
path,
this RP we'll attack.
For every day you love me,
every day I'll love you back.

83

NLP

I know there's many out there
doing fine without their sight
They get around without a fuss
in the day or in the night

They don't feel isolated
or in a crowd anxiety
Refuse to waste a second
despite the fact that they can't
see

Their world is always hazy
but their minds are always clear
The thought of future going blind
doesn't fill their nights with fear

Wish I could be more like them
but it's clear to all I'm not
I cling and hold so tightly
to the little I've still got

Although my eyes are broken
I rely on smallest hole
To keep my independence
has become my only goal

To fight to raise awareness
so my pain they understand
They won't confuse sympathy
with a welcome helping hand.

So if some days you struggle
there's no need to feel ashamed
It's the biggest hearts that hurt
the most
we're not the ones to blame

The day I lost my eyes

I felt my world would fall apart,
the day I lost my eyes.
I never thought I'd find a strength,
it caught me by surprise.

As seeing world came to an end,
my new life had begun.
I took the only option,
I had no where left to run.

The detail in the faces that I love
had disappeared,
but I still see a beauty
and this life's not all I feared.

Cause although I am blind now
and my loved ones faces lost.
Won't let this take no more of me,
no not at any cost.

I've battled all my demons,
too much time spent living scared.
So now my visions finally gone,
I know that I'm prepared.

But even still a part of me,
longs for my vision back.
I hide the pain within my heart
I'll paper over crack.

Take in the world around me,
notice things unlike before,
I'll rise to any challenge,
that for me life has in store.

I've got through all the hard times,
I've survived and wrote the book.
No matter what life throws at me,
can't be worse than what's been took.

So if you're losing sight like me,
don't worry when it's gone.
For you will have a strength in
you to help you carry on.

One Way Journey

What's it like to lose all your sight,
as yet I still don't know.
Though I've lost so much already,
I've still some way to go.

I'm on a one way journey,
just wish I could turn round.
This roads my only option,
unless a cure is found.

So for now I'm stuck in middle,
this club I don't belong.
I feel so many judging me,
but they've all got it wrong.

Cause the vision left that's useful,
can change in blink of eye.
So now I feel more distant,
as seeing days pass by.

Still I don't know how long I've
left,
till I can see no more.
I'm tired of always adjusting,
to a future blind I'm sure.

I feel my strength is slipping,
as tired eyes take dip.
I'm searching for what must be
left,
I must regain my grip.

But for now I'm stuck in darkness,
consumed by fear and doubt.
Just wish that I didn't feel alone,
just wish I could get out.

Wish I had my independence,
not on others kindness need.
I'm sick and tired of following,
Just for once I'd like to lead.

Must accept today I'm broken,
hope tomorrow soul will heal.
But today I lay here in the dark,
writing down just how I feel.

Blind inspiration

It's time I talked about,
the ones who inspire me.
The ones who came in to my life,
since I lost my fight to see.

Without them I would not be where,
I find myself right now.
I want to say my thank you's,
so stand up and take a bow.

To Molly and to Jane,
for Usher do so much.
through Molly's words and pictures,
so many hearts been touched.

She fights to raise awareness,
bring some fairness to this land.
For those who feel invisible,
she always makes a stand.

Then there's a special Geordie,
that most of you will know.
Inspired whole world with her story,
to me she's my friend Jo.

It touched the hearts of many,
when first time a voice she heard.
She spreads Usher awareness,
with each and every word.

In America there's Ramona,
who helped create my page,
She shows support believes in me,
a friend through every stage.

In the land of Oz there's Sara,
swam 12 hours to save sight.
Raising money and awareness,
to all who blindness fight.

There's lots of special people,
I now know through Stand By Me.
Speak each day though we've never met,
but one dayI hope to see.

There's Sara, Joyce and Jackie.
There's Wendy, Sherry, Jane.
Blind friends I have so many,
There's just no room to name.

You've been my inspiration,
every poem every song.
Support me to create my dream,
in print where I belong.

Just a dream

Last night I had a dream, that all
the world was blind.
So all the first impressions made,
seen only with our minds.

We'd never be distracted by the
way that people look.
Being blind would just be normal,
so no thoughts of what's been
took.

Not viewed as just disabled,
'cause we all would be the same.
So as we couldn't judge by looks,
we wouldn't feel no shame.

They'd always look beyond my
eyes,
so know the real me.
All beauty is now what's inside,
in a world where we can't see.

No need to be scared of the dark,
stay shut away in fear.
So when we'd have something to
say,
nothing to do but hear.

Be no such thing as war because
we couldn't see to kill
I wish that all the world was blind
I hope one day it will

But please don't get me wrong
don't want to take your sight
away.
Just wish we'd feel like we belong,
no burden we would lay.

So sometimes vision can deceive,
too quick to others judge.
The blind pay more attention,
to what we feel and how we
touch.

Enjoy the ride

I've lost all my peripheral,
can't see things from the side.
But now I know life's value
and each day enjoy the ride.

I see through blindness tunnel,
but I'm funnelling my strength.
The days when I felt all alone
are now thing of past tense.

With cane in hand,
I'll make my stand,
for those of us who grieve.
You may not see the positive yet,
in time you will believe.

Together we won't be alone,
although our eyes grow weak.
We may not know the answers yet,
we'll find them if we speak.

But if we lose what's left of sight,
the fight in us won't go.
There's so much more to life for us,
than vision don't you know.

Just focus on the things we have,
not on what's slipped away.
Not blind to things we're grateful for,
then it will be ok.

Though times its still frustrating,
whilst we know our sight gets
worse.
Remind yourself how you've been
blessed,
don't think you're life's been cursed.

Surround yourself with those you
love and open up your heart.
You don't need sight to feel their
love it's not too late to start.

If my eyes could see nothing

If my eyes could see nothing,
they wouldn't hurt from glare.
I wouldn't be affected by the way that people stare.

If my eyes could see nothing,
Wouldn't feel misunderstood.
Cause in their eyes I'd look just like they think a blind man should.

If my eyes could see nothing,
no need to now adjust.
In every different kind of light acceptance nows a must.

If my eyes could see nothing,
they wouldn't question me,
or think that I am lying or in search of your pity.

If my eyes could see nothing,
no longer in between,
I'd fit in to the tick box no misconception of what's seen.

If my eyes could see nothing,
they wouldn't be confused.
Relying on a thing that's broke but still no choice to use.

If my eyes could see nothing,
at night time I could sleep.
Not lay here on my pillow thinking future thoughts so deep.

If my eyes could see nothing,
perhaps be for the best.
Be no more time at hospital to fail another test.

If my eyes could see nothing,
be first in line for cure.
Then maybe in the future they'd return to how they were.

If my eyes could see nothing,
I wouldn't see the tears.
That trickle down my loved ones face, as I confront my fears.

If my eyes could see nothing,
there's so much I would miss.
Reactions on my children's face each time I hug and kiss.

If my eyes could see nothing,
I know I'd be alright.
My journey through this tunnel taught me always keep the fight.

If my eyes could see nothing,
same person I would be.
I know now that I'm so much more, than what I'm blind to see.

In the middle

RP is to many,
lots of totally different things.
The challenges are varied,
as to what this blindness brings.

There are some forever positive,
no time for bad eye days.
Refuse to waste a second,
or their tears on blur and haze.

There are some of us who live in
fear,
that can't escape the rut.
Remaining in denial,
face the truth with blind eyes
shut.

They put off thoughts preparing,
for a fate that's sure to come.
Won't admit they wear dark
glasses, cause eyes hurt from
slightest sun.

But I am in the middle,
move from bad eye days to good.
I never know what's next to come,
my knees are scarred with blood.

For every time I trip,
my confidence takes one more
knock.
I think about blind future,
when it comes it's still a shock.

But most days I am positive,
for awareness strive to fight.
I use it as a focus,
as I lose what's left of sight.

I try to help the other,
in the middle just like me.
Who sometimes lose their way,
or words to say just what they
see.

The end of seeing days

I'll take you on adventures new,
together hand in hand.
We'll sit and watch the sun go
down,
on beach of golden sands.
We'll see our children playing in,
the ocean as they swim.
But your eyes will be glistening,
before they fade to dim.

There are lots of things that one
last time,
I wish your eyes could see.
Before they all just fade from view,
because of this RP.
I'll take your hand and guide you
through,
your world of blur and haze.
To see life's beauty's one last time,
the end of seeing days.

I'll climb the highest mountain
top,
till we both reach it's peak.
For there we'll lay together,
with no words now left to speak.
A sky filled with a billion stars,
each one so bright and clear.
With one last night to count them
all,
confront our biggest fear.

There are lots of things that one
last time,
I wish your eyes could see.
Before they all just fade from view,
because of this RP.
I'll take your hand and guide you
through,
your world of blur and haze.
To see life's beauty's one last time,
the end of seeing days.

I'll take you to a secret place,
for biggest of surprise.
We'll spend the night time
dancing,
while you still have your eyes.
A party with your loved ones
there,
old friends and family.
To memorise their faces, one last
time while you can see.

There are lots of things that one
last time,
I wish your eyes could see.
Before they all just fade from view,
because of this RP.
I'll take your hand and guide you
through,
your world of blur and haze.
To see life's beauty's one last time,
the end of seeing days.

But if tomorrow blindness makes
it's way in to our life.
Just know I'll still be here for you,
forever as your wife.
I'll try my best to make it real,
ful-fill your hopes and dreams.
Just pray that I can get you there,
before blur is all that's seen.

There are lots of things that one
last time,
I wish your eyes could see.
Before they all just fade from view,
because of this RP.
I'd take your hand and guide you
through,
your world of blur and haze.
To see life's beauty's one last time,
before end of seeing days.

Blind wish

Some wish for fame and fortune
big house and fast sports cars
But I just wish to see at night,
I long to see the stars.

Some people take for granted,
their friends and family.
But I just wish my children's faces
one day more could see.

Some people wish for treasures,
like kings upon a throne.
I just wish to feel safe,
when I go out alone.

Some pin their hopes fantasies,
on dreams they can't achieve.
I just wish they wouldn't doubt
and think that we deceive.

Some wish to see the world,
It's wonders to explore.
I just wish I didn't need help,
to step outside my door.

Some people wish for diamonds,
all life's material things.
I just wish to share my words,
so true awareness brings.

Some wish for vain perfection,
a beauty that's skin deep.
I just wish I see your face,
at night each time I sleep.

Some people wish for wishes,
the more they've got they want.
But I just wish that I'll still keep,
the vision that they don't.

Our Cure

When I turned on the news today,
I heard the best surprise.
They'd took one huge step closer,
to mending our blind eyes.

The doctors and the scientists,
have said that they were sure.
For now sooner than later,
they'll announce they have our cure.

The children who have never seen,
their loving parents face.
Will soon have perfect vision,
as stem cells now replace.

All our sons and daughters,
who RP we passed on.
Will know that there's a cure for them,
so now our guilt has gone.

Outside at every hospital,
a line a million long.
Goodbye to isolation,
for now we'll all belong.

For those of us who long to drive,
behind the wheel once more.
Cause soon we'll be no longer blind
and see just like before.

That night when vision has
returned,
under a star filled sky.
We'll see in darkest darkness,
together we will lie.

A future that is nearly here,
when all the world can see.
But what of people we've
become?

How will this sight change me?
For since my eyes diminished,
more vision I have gained.
Though blind I see so clearly,
worlds beauty I've retained.

Spent years adjusting to this life,
small part now fears the change.
So when our vision comes back,
know some will find it strange.

But despite the fears that I may
have,
you'll find me in the queue.
Till then I'll be here waiting,
to see like others do.

My Story

It was only just last year you see,
when the news of blindness came.
And one thing that I knew for sure,
my life would never be the same.

The thing that hurt the most that day,
told I'd never drive again.
I knew one day get used to it,
just didn't know quite when.

My purpose in the future seemed,
to me now so unclear.
If anything was positive, then I refused to hear.

Retreated from the outside world,
for feeling vulnerable.
Affected by the brightest light,
as well as slightest dull.

Frustration grew inside me,
as the bruises they increased.
As some friends slipped away from me,
my social life deceased.

I tried to get the help I'd need,
but no one seemed to listen.
To keep a roof above our heads,
became my only mission.

To get most basic of support,
the system made me wait.
I knew that one day help would come,
and prayed it's not too late.

My wife picked up the pieces,
whilst my children looked afraid.
This blindness taking things we'd built
and future plans we'd made.

I reached out through my iPhone,
to the online community.
I didn't know these strangers,
Would soon feel like family.

I listened to their stories,
all so similar to mine.
In seeing all their struggles,
made me realise I'd be fine.

Then one night as I lay in bed,
my goal was clear to see.
Use music to open hearts and minds,
the birth of Stand By Me.

The lyrics flowed from pen to page,
poured out my fragile heart.
And instantly I knew that this,
would only be the start.

Spent each day writing poems,
for the ones who feel alone.
We'd hold hands now together,
take first steps outside our homes.

I pushed my words around the world,
in to their warm embrace.
They seemed to mean so much to them
and helped their world to face.

The messages received each day,
from all my new found friends.
Began to help my pride return,
the hole in my heart mends.

A dream I never dreamed before,
to print my words in book.
To give back all the things to us,
that this RP has took.

So here I am now asking you,
to help me change my life.
And lift the pain of blindness,
that sometimes can cut like knife.

But all the while my journey in to darkness must progress.
The symptom of this RP is,
we all see less and less.

Although my future fades now,
like the world in front of me.
I'll change how they all view us,
make them see how we all see.

I'll try to help those near and far,
who wait for distant cure.
Live for today, not worry, bout a future still unsure.

So share my words around the globe,
then one day they'll all know.
For this is the beginning and we have a way to go.

Printed in Great Britain
by Amazon.co.uk, Ltd.,
Marston Gate.